S

MAY 10 2016

DANGEROUS DRUGS

ROHYPNOL

KATE SHOUP

Cavendish
Square

New York

S

Published in 2016 by Cavendish Square Publishing, LLC
243 5th Avenue, Suite 136, New York, NY 10016

Library of Congress Cataloging-in-Publication Data

Shoup, Kate, 1972-
Rohypnol / Kate Shoup.
pages cm. — (Dangerous drugs)
Includes bibliographical references and index.
ISBN 978-1-50260-562-7 (hardcover) ISBN 978-1-50260-563-4 (ebook)
1. Flunitrazepam—Juvenile literature. I. Title.
RM666.F52S56 2016
615.7'88—dc23
2015000200

Editorial Director: David McNamara
Editor: Fletcher Doyle
Copy Editor: Rebecca Rohan
Art Director: Jeffrey Talbot
Designer: Stephanie Flecha
Senior Production Manager: Jennifer Ryder-Talbot
Production Editor: Renni Johnson
Photo Research: J8 Media

The photographs in this book are used by permission and through the courtesy of: Anuphadit/Shutterstock.com, cover,
1; Frank Micelotta/Hulton Archive/Getty Images, 4; Science & Society Picture Library/Getty Images, 9; AP Photo/
Mike Derer, 11; iStockphoto.com/Photolyric , 14; David Seed Photography/Photographer's Choice/Getty Images,
17; Designua/Shutterstock.com, 18; Merja Ojala/AFP/Getty Images 21; Edw/Shutterstock.com, 23; Photographee.
eu/Shutterstock.com, 24; Warner Bros. Pictures/Legendary Pictures/Green Hat Films/Album/Newscom, 27; Boyan
Dimitrov/Shutterstock.com, 28; Daisy-Daisy/iStock/Thinkstock, 31; John Anthony Rizzo/Stockbyte/Getty Images, ·
36; Monkey Business Images/Shutterstock.com, 39; Caiaimage/Paul Bradbury/OJO+/Getty Images, 40; AP Photo/
John Todd, 43; Laura Coles/E+/Getty Images, 46; Image Source/Getty Images, 48; Natasaadzic/iStock/Thinkstock,
50; Jennifer Steck/E+/Getty Images, 52; Wdstock/E+/Getty Images, 55; Istockphoto.com/Maica, 56.

Printed in the United States of America

Contents

CHAPTER ONE

A Powerful Tranquilizer

IN THE EARLY 1990s, KURT COBAIN WAS A famous rock singer. He was in a band called Nirvana. On March 4, 1994, Cobain's wife, musician Courtney Love, awoke to discover him on the floor of their hotel room in Rome. "He had blood coming out of his nose," she later recalled. He appeared to be in a coma. Medics rushed Cobain to the Umberto I Polyclinic Hospital, where doctors pumped his stomach. Cobain was then transferred to Rome American Hospital, where, later that day, he woke up.

According to the doctors, Cobain had experienced a drug **overdose**. Sadly, it was not the first time Cobain had used drugs. He first tried marijuana in 1980, at the age of thirteen.

Kurt Cobain of Nirvana records *MTV Unplugged in New York City* on November 18, 1993, around the time of his first overdose.

In the years that followed, he tried drugs ranging from LSD to Percodan. In 1986, Cobain used heroin for the first time. In the beginning, he used heroin only occasionally. By 1990, however, he had become addicted. It was no surprise when Cobain suffered a heroin overdose in November of 1993. He was lucky it didn't kill him.

Cobain, who grew up near Seattle, was different from many rock stars. He didn't take drugs to get high and have a good time. Instead, he took them to block out the depression he had experienced since childhood. These drugs also offered Cobain relief from intense stomach pains, which had plagued him for years. These pains were only made worse by the strain of touring with his band.

During his visit to Rome, Cobain had sought relief by taking a combination of pills that, combined with alcohol, had nearly killed him. (Some say this overdose was an attempt to commit suicide, but it's not clear whether this is true.) Among those pills was a drug called Rohypnol, which would explain his coma-like state. The drug can leave people unable to move. Cobain was lucky—this time. He survived. A month later, however, the troubled Cobain got high on heroin and shot himself in the head with a shotgun. He died on April 5, 1994, at twenty-seven years old.

The History of Rohypnol

Many drugs come from plants. For example, cocaine comes from the South American coca plant. Another example is opium. It is made from flowers called poppies. Other drugs

6

are developed, or **synthesized**, in laboratories. Rohypnol is one of these types of drugs.

Rohypnol is also known as flunitrazepam, Narcozep, Rohipnol, and Roipnol. It was synthesized in the 1970s by a Swiss company called Hoffman-La Roche. It is distributed in tablet or pill form, rather than as a liquid.

Rohypnol is a type of **benzodiazepine**. This is a kind of **psychoactive** drug. Psychoactive drugs are also called psychopharmaceuticals or psychotropics. These drugs affect brain function. They work by crossing the blood-brain barrier to act on the central nervous system (CNS). The result is a change in perception, mood, consciousness, **cognition**, and behavior. Benzodiazepines were developed to help treat people who suffer from mental health problems such as depression and anxiety.

The first benzodiazepine was a drug called chlordiazepoxide. It was developed by scientist Leo Sternbach, who worked for a company named Hoffman-La Roche. Released to the public in 1960, chlordiazepoxide, also called Librium, was a powerful **tranquilizer**. A tranquilizer is a drug used to reduce anxiety, fear, tension, and similar states of mind. Drugs of this type were commonly prescribed by **psychiatrists**. A psychiatrist is a doctor who specializes in studying, diagnosing, and treating mental illnesses, such as depression and anxiety.

The next benzodiazepine released by Hoffman-La Roche, in 1963, was also a powerful tranquilizer. This drug, called Valium, remains in wide use today. Rohypnol, which was also

Treating Mental Illness: A Brief History

In ancient times, many believed people with mental illness were possessed by evil spirits. Some people with mental illness were subjected to a treatment called "trepanning." In this procedure, doctors used stone tools to chip a hole into the patient's skull. They believed the evil spirits would leave through the hole.

In 400 BCE, the Greek physician Hippocrates (often referred to as the "father of Western medicine") realized that mental illness was a physiological condition and should be treated as such. In other words, mental illness was due to a problem with the person's body, not because of evil spirits. But he was not able to identify a cure.

In the Middle Ages, people with mental illness were cared for by their families. Later, they were placed in asylums. An **asylum** is a hospital for the mentally ill. Patients in asylums did not receive treatment for their mental illness. They were placed there to isolate them from everyone else. Often, these patients were terribly abused. Sometimes, they were even chained to walls and kept in dungeons.

During the 1700s, attitudes about the mentally ill began to change. People became more compassionate toward them. They began to believe that the mentally ill could be treated and cured. However, mistreatment of patients continued in many asylums.

In the early 1900s, psychiatrists, sometimes called "alienists," began using **psychoanalysis** to help those with mental illness. In psychoanalysis, patients talk freely about themselves—their memories, experiences, problems, and dreams.

In the 1840s, scientists developed drugs to quiet or sedate patients with mental illness. But it was not until the 1940s that drugs were used effectively to treat these patients. Today, there are many drugs used to treat mental illness. Thanks to these drugs, many who suffer from mental illness go on to live full, rich lives.

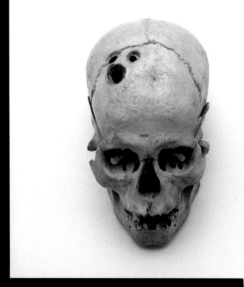

The skull of a person who was subjected to trepanning about four thousand years ago.

9

developed by Leo Sternbach, is similar to Valium. However, it is seven to ten times as strong. Rohypnol is made of the chemicals carbon, hydrogen, fluorine, nitrogen, and oxygen.

Initially, benzodiazepines were embraced by the public. Soon, however, concern grew about the long-term effects of these drugs. Even so, Rohypnol was widely used in more than sixty countries, including countries in Europe and Latin America. However, it has never been approved for manufacture or sale by the United States Food and Drug Administration (FDA). This is because of the drug's **potency**, or strength. It is also because Rohypnol is known to cause physical and psychological dependence. The use of Rohypnol can also result in the development of benzodiazepine **withdrawal** syndrome. Although Rohypnol is not approved for sale in the United States, many other benzodiazepines are.

In the United States, Rohypnol is classified as a Schedule IV drug. It is illegal to buy, sell, or possess Schedule IV drugs without a **prescription**. (A prescription is an order from a doctor or healthcare worker that authorizes a patient to receive a certain medicine or treatment.) Even with a prescription, it is impossible to buy Rohypnol in the United States. Only those who have legally purchased the drug outside the country are permitted to have it.

REPORTS OF MISUSE

After the release of Rohypnol in the 1970s, reports of its misuse quickly surfaced, particularly in Europe. By 1990, the misuse of Rohypnol had emerged in the US. As the abuse of

Chemist Leo Sternbach, seated in front of his wife, Herta, was the first person to synthesize Rohypnol. He also invented Valium.

WHAT ARE DRUG SCHEDULES?

Drugs are grouped into five categories. These are called schedules. The schedule to which a drug is assigned depends on a few factors. One factor is the drug's intended medical use. Another is the likelihood of someone becoming dependent on it. The most important is the rate at which the drug is abused.

In the United States, the schedules are as follows:

- **Schedule I:** These drugs have no accepted medical use and a high potential for abuse. Examples of these drugs are heroin and LSD.
- **Schedule II:** These drugs have a high potential for abuse, but unlike Schedule I drugs, have an accepted medical use. Examples are cocaine, morphine, oxycodone, and Adderall (the brand name for a combination of amphetamine and dextroamphetamine).
- **Schedule III:** These drugs have a medical use and have less potential for abuse than Schedule I and II drugs. Nevertheless, it is possible to become physically

and psychologically addicted to Schedule III drugs. Examples are Vicodin and some barbiturates.

- **Schedule IV:** These drugs are weaker and less addictive than Schedule III drugs. Still, they are addictive, and their effects should not be underestimated. Examples are Xanax and Rohypnol.
- **Schedule V:** These drugs have a low potential for abuse compared to drugs in other schedules, but the potential does exist. Examples include cough medicines with codeine.

The US Drug Enforcement Agency (DEA) classifies Rohypnol as a Schedule IV drug because it is legally prescribed elsewhere. However, the penalties for possessing, handling, or distributing it are the same as the penalties for a Schedule I drug, such as heroin. Those found with the drug can receive up to three years in prison and a fine of $5,000. In addition, Rohypnol has been classified as a Schedule III drug in other countries.

Rohypnol is sometimes called a "club drug" because of its use at places such as nightclubs.

Rohypnol became more widespread, it began to be known by other "street" names. The most common of these was "roofies." The drug was also called "roach," "roopies," "rope," "ruffies," and "whiteys," among other names. In addition,

14

Rohypnol—along with drugs like MDMA (ecstasy), GHB, methamphetamine, and LSD—was sometimes called a "club drug." This is because it was often used at bars, nightclubs, concerts, and parties.

Though still illegal, Rohypnol remains widely available in the United States. Drug smugglers bring Rohypnol or generic versions of the drug into the United States from Mexico and other countries. Rohypnol is also relatively inexpensive. It usually costs about $5 per tablet. Because of its wide availability and relatively low cost, Rohypnol is very popular among young people. In fact, teenagers and young adults ages thirteen to thirty are the primary users of Rohypnol. Generally, males use Rohypnol more than females.

Rohypnol is often found on high school and college campuses. According to a recent study in the US, 0.4 percent of eighth graders had used Rohypnol in the past year, as had 0.4 percent of tenth graders and 1 percent of twelfth graders. Although these numbers were higher a few years ago (in 1997, they were 1 percent, 1.3 percent, and 1.6 percent, respectively), the use of Rohypnol by school-age children remains a serious problem.

CHAPTER TWO

Applying the Brain's Brakes

ROHYPNOL IS A TYPE OF BENZODIAZEPINE. Benzodiazepines are a form of psychoactive drug. These drugs affect brain function by crossing the blood-brain barrier to act on the central nervous system (CNS). The result is a change in perception, mood, consciousness, cognition, and behavior.

To understand how benzodiazepines like Rohypnol work, it's important to know a few things about the brain. Nerve cells called neurons are the building blocks of the brain. These cells process and transmit information through electrical and chemical signals. Attached to neurons are axons. These are like wires. On these wires are chemical messengers, called neurotransmitters. Neurotransmitters carry electrical and chemical signals from the body of the nerve cell to the end of the axon. There, they are released to interact with other

Rohypnol is not legal in the United States, but it is still widely abused here.

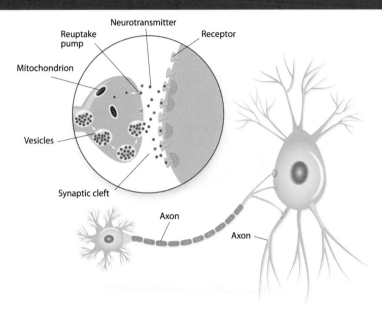

STRUCTURE OF A TYPICAL CHEMICAL SYNAPSE

Neurotransmitter

Reuptake pump

Mitochondrion

Receptor

Vesicles

Synaptic cleft

Axon

Axon

Rohypnol and other drugs alter the way the central nervous system works.

neurons. Receptors on these other neurons, called dendrites, receive the neurotransmitters. There are different receptors for different types of neurotransmitters. A neurotransmitter and dendrite "fit" the way the right key fits into a lock.

There are many types of neurotransmitters—more than one hundred in all. More and more are discovered each year. Each neurotransmitter has its own important action, or job. For example, a neurotransmitter called dopamine causes feelings of pleasure and motivation. Another neurotransmitter, called serotonin, helps to regulate appetite, sleep, mood,

18

and more. A third neurotransmitter, called norepinephrine, relates to sleep patterns, focus, and alertness.

Benzodiazepines, including Rohypnol, work by boosting the action of a neurotransmitter called gamma-aminobutyric acid (GABA). GABA is the brain's major inhibitory neurotransmitter. In other words, its job is to reduce brain activity to slow or calm things down. Benzodiazepines reduce this brain activity even further, slowing or calming things down even more.

If someone uses a benzodiazepine like Rohypnol on a regular basis, the brain begins to produce less GABA. That makes it harder for people who use the drug to achieve the pleasurable effects they desire. They must use more of the drug to create the same feeling. When someone needs more of a drug to achieve the same results, he or she is said to have developed a **tolerance** for the drug. When someone develops a tolerance for a drug, it's easy to become addicted to it.

Legitimate Uses

Rohypnol is similar to a drug called Valium, but is seven to ten times stronger. It is typically distributed in tablet form.

Rohypnol has many legitimate uses. These include the following:

Hypnotic: The word "hypnotic" comes from the Greek *hypnos*, or sleep. A hypnotic, then, is a type of drug that helps patients to sleep. Rohypnol is used as a short-term treatment for insomnia, or sleeplessness. It is also used as a surgical anesthetic. That is, doctors give it to patients before operations to knock them out.

Sedative: A sedative, also called a tranquilizer, is a type of drug that calms the user. Rohypnol is sometimes used for this purpose. Sedatives work by reducing irritability or excitement. A doctor might prescribe a sedative for a patient who is experiencing alarm about an upcoming medical procedure. Or, a doctor might prescribe a sedative for someone who is unable to calm down after experiencing a traumatic event. Sedatives are typically taken in very low doses.

Anxiolytic: Rohypnol sometimes acts as an anxiolytic. An anxiolytic is a type of drug that reduces short-term anxiety. Anxiolytics are also used to treat anxiety disorders.

Anticonvulsant: Some doctors prescribe Rohypnol as an anticonvulsant. An anticonvulsant is a drug used to treat people who suffer from seizures. A seizure, sometimes called a "fit," is a sudden and brief attack that occurs as a result of abnormal electrical activity in the brain. When someone experiences a seizure, the person's body often convulses, or shakes rapidly and uncontrollably. Or, the person's body might "seize up," or stiffen—hence the name "seizure." Rohypnol helps to combat this.

Muscle relaxant: Rohypnol is also used as a muscle relaxant. A muscle relaxant is a drug that eases muscle spasms and muscle pain.

What Rohypnol Looks Like

In the 1970s, when Rohypnol was first released, it was distributed as a small, white pill. Initially, these pills were available in doses of 1 or 2 milligrams. However, due to the drug's potency, most countries began limiting the dosage to 1 milligram. Beginning in 1997, the company that manufactures Rohypnol (originally called Hoffman-La Roche, but now called Roche) changed the pill's appearance. This was because some criminals were known to place the drug in people's drinks to render them unconscious. Rohypnol is now an olive green tablet that has a speckled blue core. This core acts as a dye. If this pill is placed in a clear or light-colored liquid, it will dye the liquid blue and leave a green residue. However, generic versions of the pill may not contain this blue dye. Rohypnol is typically packaged in foil-backed bubble packs.

Rohypnol is now formulated as an olive-green tablet with a blue dye inside.

Sometimes, Rohypnol is used in psychiatric therapy settings. The drug helps patients to relax and to lower their **inhibitions**. This **enables** them to talk more openly with their therapists.

Rohypnol is illegal in the United States. However, many other countries allow its use, despite its dangers. For example, it is available with a prescription in Australia, Germany, Norway, and Sweden, and in many countries in Latin America.

Why People Abuse Rohypnol

People abuse Rohypnol for the same reason they abuse any other drug: to get high. According to those who have used the drug, Rohypnol makes them feel relaxed and at ease. Their anxieties disappear. It lowers their inhibitions, causing them to act in ways they might not otherwise. People on Rohypnol may also experience a sense of fearlessness.

On Rohypnol, users become extremely intoxicated—and quickly. The drug's effects are similar to those of alcohol. After just a small dose, the user may have difficulty standing or speaking. A dose as small as 1 mg can affect a person for eight to twelve hours. One important aspect of Rohypnol is that its use often results in **amnesia**, or memory loss. Those who use Rohypnol often do not remember experiences they had while under the influence of the drug. Rohypnol can also cause the user to lose consciousness.

Some people are attracted to drugs like Rohypnol because they like the idea of experiencing a thrilling and unpredictable rush. For some, the drug makes them feel more confident and

Rohypnol can cause the user to lose consciousness for hours.

self-assured. Others are intrigued by the danger associated with using the drug. Kids may fall prey to Rohypnol due to peer pressure. If "everyone is doing it," then kids might feel like they should, too. Or they might use the drug as a kind of a crutch, to help them cope with problems in their daily lives. (Of course, Rohypnol only makes most problems even more difficult to solve.) However, there are no good reasons to abuse Rohypnol.

How People Abuse Rohypnol

People abuse Rohypnol in a variety of ways. Sometimes, people simply swallow a Rohypnol tablet. Other times, they crush the tablet and use a straw to inhale the resulting powder. Some users might dissolve a crushed tablet in a

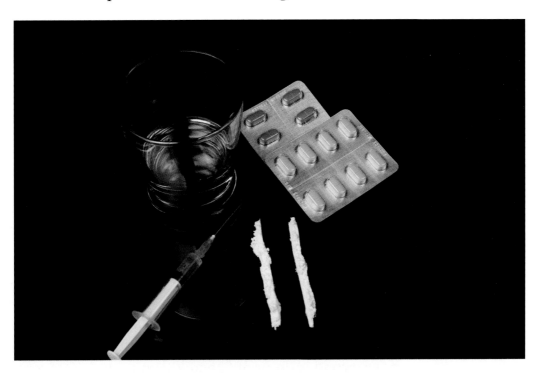

There are many ways to abuse Rohypnol. All of them have their added dangers.

beverage and drink it. (Criminals will spike the drink of their intended victim with Rohypnol to disable them.) Or, they might dissolve a crushed tablet in liquid and use a syringe, or needle, to inject it into their bloodstream. This approach is particularly dangerous.

Regardless of how the drug is consumed, its effect is very powerful—and fast. In fact, the effects of Rohypnol can be felt within fifteen to thirty minutes. The effects of the drug typically peak within two to three hours, and can linger for eight hours or more. The more Rohypnol a person consumes, the stronger its effects. Someone who has taken Rohypnol will appear drunk. The person might have trouble standing or slur his or her speech. Because the drug slows the pulse and breathing, the user might pass out, or even die.

Often, Rohypnol is consumed with other mind-altering substances. For example, some users mix Rohypnol with alcohol. This helps to boost their high. Other users take it with heroin, for a sedative effect. Finally, some users take Rohypnol to combat the withdrawal effects associated with other drugs. Of course, using Rohypnol in this way simply replaces one problem with another.

CHAPTER THREE

Risky Business

IN 2009, WARNER BROS. RELEASED A MOVIE called *The Hangover*. It told the story of four men who traveled to Las Vegas for a bachelor party. The morning after they arrive, three of the men awaken in their hotel suite. They have no memory of what happened the night before. They also cannot explain why one of the men is missing, why the suite is in a complete disarray, where one of the men's front tooth went, why there is a tiger in the bathroom, why there is a chicken in the living room, or who the baby in their closet is. The rest of the movie is dedicated to solving these mysteries.

At the heart of the movie is one dangerous detail: the men had unknowingly taken Rohypnol. This explains why they had no memory of the events from the night before. Although the movie is a comedy, if such a scenario were

Ed Helms from the movie *The Hangover*, in which the main characters take Rohypnol by accident.

A Rohypnol hangover is particularly painful.

28

to unfold in real life, it would be far from funny. The fact is, although some people may enjoy the high provided by Rohypnol, it is a very dangerous drug.

Short-Term Effects

Someone who has taken Rohypnol will likely look and act as if they are drunk. Here are other symptoms that a person on Rohypnol might experience:

- Loss of muscle control
- Difficulty with motor movements
- Vision problems
- Dizziness
- Nausea or other stomach problems, such as vomiting
- Confusion
- Reduced judgment
- Reduced levels of consciousness
- Blackout
- Sleepiness

Rohypnol doesn't just affect the body when it is in the user's system. It also affects the body after it wears off. The after-effects of Rohypnol are similar to those of alcohol—often called a **hangover**. Symptoms of a hangover may include drowsiness, headache, dizziness, and nausea. For many, a Rohypnol hangover is worse than a hangover from any other drug. This is because of Rohypnol's strong sedating effects. The symptoms of a Rohypnol hangover typically begin within twenty-four hours and can last for forty-eight hours.

LONG-TERM EFFECTS

Long-term Rohypnol users may experience any number of adverse effects. One of these is an impairment of cognition, including sustained attention, verbal learning, and memory. Another is poor sleep or sleep disorders. Other effects include:

- Nausea
- Headaches
- Dizziness
- Irritability
- Lethargy
- Personality changes
- Aggression

Some long-term users of benzodiazepines like Rohypnol experience a decline in mental health. In particular, long-time users of Rohypnol are at risk for developing chronic depression. Ironically, even though benzodiazepines, including Rohypnol, are often used to combat anxiety, long-term use can cause an increase in anxiety for some users.

As a Schedule IV drug, Rohypnol may be considered weaker and less addictive than drugs in Schedules I, II, or III. This doesn't mean you won't become physically and psychologically addicted to it. In fact, Rohypnol is one of the most addictive of all benzodiazepines.

Physical addiction happens when a person's body starts to depend on a drug. If the drug is removed, the person will feel an intense physical reaction. (This reaction is called

ROHYPNOL RISKS

Chronic depression is similar to regular depression. However, it lasts longer—two years or more. Chronic depression is also called dysthymia. People who suffer from chronic depression experience a prolonged state of low mood. That is, they are unhappy for a long time. For example, they may feel sad, anxious, empty, hopeless, helpless, worthless, guilty, irritable, or restless. Many people with chronic depression lose interest in activities that were once enjoyable. For example, someone who used to enjoy playing tennis might stop playing if he or she develops chronic depression. People with chronic depression may also experience insomnia, excessive sleeping, or fatigue, as well as a loss of appetite. Many people who experience chronic depression have thoughts of suicide, and may even attempt the act. According to the 1999 White House Conference on Mental Health, depression is the cause of more than two-thirds of reported suicides in the US.

Chronic depression may result from long-term use of Rohypnol.

withdrawal.) Psychological addiction happens when someone becomes mentally or emotionally attached to using a drug. If the drug is removed, the person feels quite anxious. This is a psychological reaction rather than a biological one.

Often, people become both physically and psychologically addicted to a drug. This is often the case with Rohypnol. Not only does the person's body require the drug to feel good, but he or she has an emotional connection to using it, too. Overcoming these addictions is very difficult.

Regular Rohypnol users may develop a tolerance for the drug. That means the user must consume more and more of the drug to get high. This occurs because the GABA receptors in the user's brain become desensitized. When someone develops a tolerance for Rohypnol, it increases the chances that he or she will become addicted to the drug. A user can begin to develop a tolerance for Rohypnol within days or weeks of first taking the drug. The longer a person takes Rohypnol, the more likely it is he or she will become dependent on it or addicted to it.

If someone does become addicted to Rohypnol, that person will likely experience withdrawal if he or she attempts to stop taking the drug. Symptoms of withdrawal can include seizures, psychosis, severe insomnia, and severe anxiety. Often, someone who is addicted to Rohypnol will continue taking the drug just to avoid experiencing these unpleasant symptoms.

Signs of Addiction

How can you tell if someone is addicted to Rohypnol? Here are a few behaviors to look out for:

- Having a preoccupation with the drug
- Having to use more of the drug to get high
- Having difficulty controlling the use of the drug
- Sneaking around or being secretive
- Hiding the use of the drug
- Spending excessive amounts of money on the drug
- Using the drug as a means of escape
- Using the drug instead of doing other activities
- Missing school or work to do drugs
- Continuing to use the drug, in spite of its harmful effects
- Having an inability to cope without the drug
- Having an inability to quit using the drug

There are also many physical signs of addiction. These include the following:

- Drowsiness or lethargy
- Impaired motor coordination
- Slurred speech
- Amnesia or memory problems
- Confusion
- Mood swings

- Nausea and vomiting
- Headaches
- Tremors

If you or someone you know shows any of these signs, it is cause for concern. Suicide is a common outcome when someone is addicted to a benzodiazepine, like Rohypnol.

A tool called the "Benzodiazepine Dependence Self-Report Questionnaire," or "Bendep-SRQ" for short, can also help to show if someone has developed an addiction to a benzodiazepine, such as Rohypnol. The questionnaire is available at cckan.ruhosting.nl/benengli.htm.

Overdose Dangers

One of the most significant dangers of the use of Rohypnol is overdose. An overdose occurs when someone consumes more of a drug than his or her body can handle. How much Rohypnol is needed to cause an overdose? The answer to this is different for each person. However, anyone who uses Rohypnol is at risk of an overdose.

Signs of Rohypnol overdose typically develop within four hours of taking the drug. These signs include the following:

- Excessive sedation
- Slowed heart rate
- Lowered blood pressure
- Nausea
- Vomiting

- Confusion
- Impaired judgment
- Dizziness
- Blurred vision
- Slurred speech
- Unsteady walking

A more serious overdose could result in respiratory depression. Respiratory depression is a slowing of the breathing. This results in a buildup of carbon dioxide in the blood. A serious overdose could also cause memory loss, loss of consciousness, or coma.

Sometimes, an overdose of Rohypnol can lead to death. A 1993 study in Great Britain showed that of all the benzodiazepines, Rohypnol was the most likely to cause death. Even when death does not occur, someone who has overdosed on Rohypnol is in danger. This is because the symptoms of an overdose—particularly a serious one—may make it impossible for the user to fend off an attacker or other threat. And because Rohypnol often causes memory loss, he or she may have no memory of what has occurred.

Often, overdoses happen because the user forgets how much of the drug he or she has already taken. For example, a user who has taken four pills might believe he has taken only one or two and assume it is safe to take another. Another reason for overdose is that not all doses are the same. This is a problem in the United States, where pills are obtained illegally and not subject to government regulation. A third

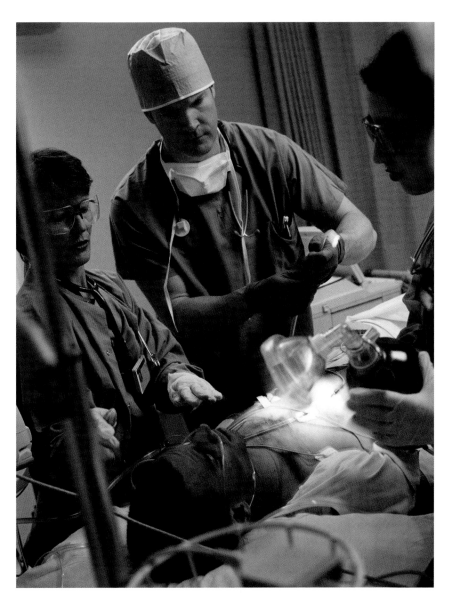

The use of Rohypnol can result in loss of consciousness, coma, or even death.

cause has to do with the delivery method. Typically, Rohypnol is consumed orally, or through the mouth. But if, for example, the pill is crushed and the resulting powder is inhaled or injected, it could result in a stronger-than-normal amount of the drug in one's system. Finally, the effects of Rohypnol are magnified when mixed with alcohol or other drugs, which increases the chances of an overdose. Alcohol increases the toxic effect of the drug. It is also an inhibitor, so using it with Rohypnol is like taking a double dose. Two inhibitors can combine to shut down the body's functions, resulting in death. Someone who slips the drug into another person's drink is putting that person's life in danger. The bottom line is that any amount of Rohypnol can be dangerous.

If someone experiences an overdose, he or she should be taken to a doctor right away. In some cases, a doctor might give the patient a drug called flumazenil as an **antidote**. Either way, it's critical that a health professional cares for the patient until the danger has passed.

CHAPTER FOUR

Hidden Dangers

ROHYPNOL DOESN'T JUST HARM THE USER'S body. It can cause lots of other problems. These range from the financial to the criminal. In addition, there are several hidden dangers to using the drug.

Like any illegal drug, Rohypnol costs money. Usually, pills cost about $5 each. If you develop a drug habit, you could easily find yourself spending $50 to $100 per week on the drug. When you are a student with a limited income, this adds up fast.

But there is another financial ramification to using this drug. Because Rohypnol impairs the user's judgment, he or she may spend money while on the drug without realizing it. Add to this the fact that if someone becomes addicted to Rohypnol, it is unlikely that he or she will be able to hold a job. With no money coming in—and a costly drug habit—one could quickly find oneself in serious financial trouble.

Criminals may place Rohypnol in the drink of their unsuspecting victim.

Rohypnol and Robbery

Although many people use Rohypnol to become high themselves, some criminals give it to others without their knowledge or consent. Often, these criminals then assault

Rohypnol causes short-term memory loss, leaving users disoriented when they awaken.

the impaired person. Sometimes, this assault is in the form of a robbery. The criminal will steal the impaired person's wallet, purse, jewelry, or other personal possessions.

Usually, the scenario is as follows: The criminal places a large dose of the drug in the drink of his or her unsuspecting victim, usually at a bar or club. Because the drug is odorless, tasteless, and often colorless, the victim does not detect it in the drink. Despite the efforts of the company that manufactures Rohypnol to make it visible when dissolved in liquid, change may not be visible in darker-colored drinks, in drinks served in an opaque container, or in environments where the lighting is low. In addition, generic versions of the pill may still lack the dye that will discolor liquids. After consuming the spiked beverage, the victim becomes sedated or incapacitated, unable to resist or defend himself or herself against a robbery. In addition, because Rohypnol often results in amnesia, the victim may have only a limited—or even no—recollection of the event. This makes it difficult for the victim to remember who robbed them—or that they were robbed at all.

One California businessman, Simon Garcia, experienced this type of robbery while on a business trip in Hong Kong, China. He went out with some friends and colleagues on a Friday night. "The next thing I knew," he told *Marie Claire* magazine, "it was 2 a.m. on Sunday, and I was lying on my bed … My cell phone, wallet, and $3,000 Omega watch were gone." Also gone was Garcia's memory of the previous twenty-four hours.

ROHYPNOL AND RAPE

Although criminals do use Rohypnol to commit robbery, it's more common for them to use it to commit rape. As with the robbery scenario, the criminal simply spikes the drink of his intended victim with a large dose of Rohypnol. Often, the dose used is enough to knock the victim out. While the victim is incapacitated, the criminal will rape him or her. Typically, the victim will remember little—if anything—about the event. For this reason, Rohypnol is often called a "date-rape drug."

Rohypnol is not the only drug used to commit rape (or robbery) in this way. There are other date-rape drugs. One is called gamma hydroxybutyric acid, or GHB. GHB is a Schedule I controlled substance. Although it is not a benzodiazepine, GHB has many of the same effects as Rohypnol. Not surprisingly, criminals use GHB the same way they do Rohypol: by pouring it into someone's drink and then assaulting him or her once the drug's sedative effects have kicked in. Like Rohypnol, GHB is odorless and often colorless. However, it has an extremely salty taste. This explains why it is sometimes called "salt water." It also goes by the names "G-juice," "soap," and "vita-G." Another so-called date-rape drug is ketamine. This drug, sometimes called "special K," "black hole," and "super acid," has legitimate medical purposes. It is used mainly for anesthetic purposes. However, like Rohypnol, its use results in memory loss, making it attractive to criminals who want to sedate their victims.

Combating Date-Rape Drugs

Students at North Carolina State University have developed a nail polish that can detect the presence of date rape drugs such as Rohypnol and GHB. The nail polish, called Undercover Colors, changes color when it comes into contact with these substances. "With our nail polish," the inventors say, "any woman will be empowered to discreetly ensure her safety by simply stirring her drink with her finger." Their hope is to "make potential perpetrators afraid to spike a woman's drink because there's now a risk that they can get caught." Another method for stopping would-be attackers has been developed by a company called Drink Safe Technologies. This company manufactures special drink coasters that detect the presence of some date rape drugs, including GHB and Ketamine (although not Rohypnol). Just one drop of a drink on the coaster will indicate whether the drink has been spiked.

Special drink coasters detect the presence of some date rape drugs.

How often do predators use Rohypnol and other date rape drugs in their attempts to sexually assault unwitting victims? It's difficult to say. Often, if a date rape drug has been used, the victim's memory of the event is hazy at best. In fact, the victim may never realize that he or she has been the victim of a sexual assault. Even if the victim becomes aware an assault has taken place, it may not be until after the effects of the drug wear off. By then, the drug may be difficult to detect. Occasionally, law-enforcement officers get lucky—like the time they were able to arrest Mark Perez. According to *Newsweek* magazine, "Perez, a satellite-dish installer from Pembroke Pines, FL, couldn't resist boasting to friends that he'd drugged and raped a dozen women, most of whom he had picked up in bars." (Perez pleaded no contest to one count of sexually battering a helpless person and received an eight-year prison sentence in 1995.) Typically, however, these crimes go unreported. For this reason, it is difficult to determine how frequently Rohypnol and other date-rape drugs are used in this way.

How can you protect yourself from being given Rohypnol or another date rape drug without your knowledge or consent? Here are a few tips:

- Pay attention to what's going on around you. Be aware.
- Never accept a drink from someone else—even someone you know.
- Open all containers yourself.

- Keep your drink with you at all times. If you realize you've left your drink unattended, pour it out.
- Don't share your drink with someone else.
- Don't drink from a punch bowl or similar open container.
- If your drink smells or tastes strange, don't drink it.

Here are some signs you might have been drugged:

- You feel drunk, but you haven't consumed any alcohol.
- You wake up feeling very hung over.
- You have no memory of a period of time.
- You remember having a drink, but do not remember anything after that point.
- Your clothes are torn, or are not put on correctly—and you don't know why.

If the signs point to you having been drugged and raped, get help right away. Call 911 or ask someone to take you to a hospital emergency room. As soon as you arrive, explain that you believe you may have been raped and ask the hospital to take a urine sample that can be used to test for date rape drugs. The hospital will use a "rape kit" to collect evidence. To ensure that all possible evidence is collected, do not urinate, bathe, brush your teeth, wash your hands, change clothes, eat, or drink before you go to the hospital. Also, do not clean the area where you think the crime may have occurred in case evidence has been left behind. While you are at the hospital, call the police. Tell them exactly what you remember—even if that means admitting you were doing drugs or drinking alcohol. Once the initial crisis has passed, seek counseling. A counselor can help you work through the feelings of shame, guilt, fear, and shock that may follow. For help finding a counselor, try calling the National Sexual Assault Hotline at (800) 656-HOPE.

ROHYPNOL AND VIOLENCE

Sometimes, Rohypnol users experience **paradoxical effects**. These are symptoms that are opposite of what a user would normally experience. In some cases, rather than experiencing

Some criminals take Rohypnol to increase their confidence before committing crimes.

a sedative effect, users instead become more aggressive. These users may even become violent. According to an organization called the Rohypnol Addiction Center, "Users can become ruthless, coldblooded, and aggressive, yet have no recollection of the acts they committed in an impaired state." The Rohypnol Addiction Center goes on to say, "They may feel an inflated sense of personal power, reduced feelings of insecurity, and a feeling of invincibility."

Some criminals take Rohypnol before they commit crimes. This results in a lack of inhibition and increases their confidence. Also, because Rohypnol often results in amnesia, it is difficult for police to question them if they are caught.

Hidden Dangers

Not all of the dangers associated with Rohypnol use are obvious. For example, if someone injects Rohypnol, it could result in vein inflammation or blood clots. Worse, if the user shares the needle with someone else, he or she could catch hepatitis or even human immunodeficiency virus (HIV).

Because Rohypnol results in a lack of inhibition, it may increase the likelihood of someone having unprotected sex. This can lead to any number of health problems. These include catching sexually transmitted diseases. Or, a woman could become pregnant before she is ready.

Rohypnol is illegal in the United States, so no government agency regulates it. This gives drug dealers an opportunity to sell poorly made knockoffs. These knockoffs may be even more dangerous than the real thing.

Someone on Rohypnol is far too impaired to drive.

Rohypnol affects the user's motor control, so they are more likely to fall and incur an injury such as a broken bone. A user is also in no state to operate a motor vehicle. Driving while under the influence of Rohypnol can easily result in a traffic accident, causing severe injury or even death.

CHAPTER FIVE

Rohypnol Recovery

IF YOU THINK SOMEONE YOU CARE ABOUT is abusing Rohypnol, it is important to speak up. His or her life may be on the line! Do not be surprised, however, if the person denies that he or she has a problem. In that case, an **intervention** may be necessary. An intervention is when loved ones gather together to talk to the user about his or her problem. Often, they talk about the ways in which the user's behavior has hurt them. The goal of the intervention is not to embarrass the drug user. Rather, it is to encourage him or her to seek help.

Help can come in many forms. A doctor can help the user address any health issues that may have arisen due to his or her Rohypnol use or advise the user on the best plan of treatment. Help is also available from school counselors, drug counselors, hotlines, and the Internet.

Get help to put yourself on the road to recovery.

Treatment Programs

People with a serious drug problem may need to go to **rehab**. There are many types of rehab. The type you choose depends on the situation. One option is an inpatient rehab program. With this type of program, the patient stays at a hospital or other treatment facility for a period of time. This program is best for someone who is battling a long-term addiction, faces an immediate health risk, or has recently experienced

50

an overdose. It enables caregivers to oversee the patient's mental and physical well-being around the clock. Inpatient programs usually last thirty days, although some are longer or shorter. For patients experiencing withdrawal symptoms, this type of treatment is best.

Another option is an outpatient program. People in outpatient programs live at home, but make regular visits to a hospital or other facility for treatment to address their addiction. This type of program works well for people who have a history of drug use, but are not in immediate danger or experiencing serious withdrawal symptoms. Outpatient programs are also helpful for patients who have completed an inpatient program, but need more treatment.

Some rehab programs prescribe physical activity to help patients relax and reduce their stress. In addition, almost all rehab programs involve some type of therapy. In therapy, patients talk to a drug counselor about why they began using drugs. Patients also work with drug counselors to develop strategies for avoiding drugs in the future. Often, this involves identifying and avoiding triggers. A **trigger** is something that causes something else to happen—in this case, something that causes the patient to want to use drugs. One common trigger for drug users is the company of fellow users. Another is a place, such as a club, where they used drugs. Stress is also a common trigger.

No two people are alike, and no two treatment plans are, either. What works best for one person may not work for another. When overcoming drug addiction—whether

HOLDING AN INTERVENTION

An intervention can be an emotional experience. Here are some guidelines for holding a successful one:

- Make sure the right people attend. Do not include anyone who has had a hand in enabling the drug user.
- It's important not to overwhelm the addict. Only one person should speak at a time. Give the abuser the opportunity to respond. Also, remain calm. Do not become overly emotional.

If someone denies he or she is using Rohypnol, an intervention may be necessary.

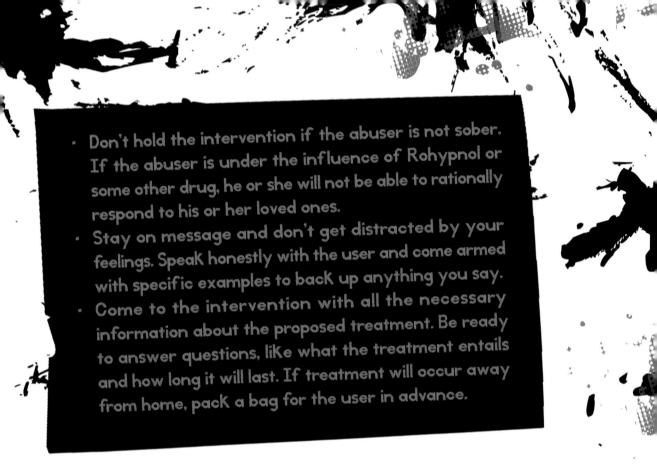

- Don't hold the intervention if the abuser is not sober. If the abuser is under the influence of Rohypnol or some other drug, he or she will not be able to rationally respond to his or her loved ones.
- Stay on message and don't get distracted by your feelings. Speak honestly with the user and come armed with specific examples to back up anything you say.
- Come to the intervention with all the necessary information about the proposed treatment. Be ready to answer questions, like what the treatment entails and how long it will last. If treatment will occur away from home, pack a bag for the user in advance.

for Rohypnol or some other substance—an individualized treatment plan works best. This plan should take into account the severity of the addiction, the likelihood of withdrawal symptoms, medical conditions or complications, the patient's emotional state, the patient's willingness to participate, the potential for relapse, and the patient's living situation.

Following an individualized plan helps patients to beat their addiction and reclaim their lives. Overcoming any kind of drug addiction takes courage and determination. Rohypnol is no exception. Anyone attempting to stop using Rohypnol is sure to experience difficult moments. But with commitment and the right treatment plan, many people succeed.

Benzodiazepine Withdrawal Syndrome

Rohypnol users who have become dependent on the drug (or to any other benzodiazepine) may experience benzodiazepine withdrawal syndrome when they stop taking the drug. Symptoms of this syndrome, sometimes called "benzo withdrawal," include the following:

- Aches and pains
- Agitation and restlessness
- Anxiety
- Blurred or double vision
- Chest pain
- Cognitive difficulty
- Depression
- Dizziness
- Fatigue
- Gastrointestinal problems (including nausea, vomiting, dry retching, and diarrhea)
- Headache
- High blood pressure
- Lack of concentration
- Memory loss
- Muscular pain and stiffness
- Palpitations

With commitment and the right treatment plan, it is possible to live drug free.

- Panic attacks
- Problems sleeping (including insomnia and nightmares)
- Sweating
- Tremors
- Weight loss

In addition, more serious symptoms can develop. This is especially true if the patient stops using the drug abruptly or if he or she has used the drug for a long time. These include coma, convulsions, delusions, hallucinations, psychosis, and seizures. The person may become violent or even try suicide.

Someone experiencing benzodiazepine withdrawal syndrome should have his or her health monitored.

While you might think these withdrawal symptoms would steadily decrease with the passage of time, this is not always the case. Often, the symptoms become stronger and weaker in a cyclical or random fashion. Substances like caffeine can also worsen these symptoms.

To manage these symptoms, it's best to have the person detox gradually by progressively lowering the dose. This should be done under the supervision of a medical professional. The addict should not quit cold turkey as this can harm his or her central nervous system and lower the person's chances of success. Chances of success are also improved by reassurance from family, friends, counselors, and peers that the user's symptoms—while painful—are both normal and temporary. It may well be that a rehab or detox facility is the best place for the user during withdrawal, particularly during the first three to five days.

How long will a user experience withdrawal symptoms? It depends. How quickly the user has gone off the drug is one factor. Another is how long the user took the drug. Genetic factors may also come into play. For the unlucky few, benzo withdrawal can persist for months or even years. Typically, this happens only to long-term users of the drug. Gradually lessening the dose rather than quitting cold turkey can help prevent this from occurring. If a user does experience a protracted withdrawal, doctors may prescribe a medication called flumazenil. It helps to reverse a user's tolerance for the drug and to minimize symptoms of withdrawal.

Eventually, assuming the user remains free of the drug, these withdrawal symptoms will subside. When that occurs, and the drug is completely out of their system, patients often find that their physical and mental health are improved, their mood elevated, and their learning abilities enhanced.

EDUCATION AND AWARENESS

The best way to avoid the dangers of Rohypnol is to never use it in the first place. Sometimes, however, it may be difficult to "just say no." Knowing the facts about Rohypnol can help people choose not to use.

To that end, education and awareness are critical. Anyone can help spread awareness—even kids. One way to spread awareness is to design posters or flyers that explain what Rohypnol is and what it does to the body. The poster could include warning signs to look for as well as the phone number or web address for a local treatment center. Another way to increase awareness is to arrange a neighborhood or town meeting. This meeting could feature a guest speaker, such as a police officer, drug counselor, or even a former addict. These individuals could share information and tips to help stop or prevent Rohypnol abuse.

GLOSSARY

amnesia Memory loss, including events over just a few hours.

antidote A medicine taken to counteract another drug or a poison.

asylum A special hospital for the mentally ill.

benzodiazepine A kind of psychoactive drug that has a tranquilizing effect.

cognition The process of acquiring knowledge and understanding.

enable To make it possible or even easier for someone to do something.

hangover The after-effects of drinking alcohol or taking certain drugs. Symptoms may include drowsiness, headache, dizziness, and nausea.

inhibition A feeling of self-consciousness which keeps people from doing things.

intervention An event during which loved ones gather together to talk to a drug user.

overdose Occurs when someone consumes more of a drug than his or her body can handle.

paradoxical effects Symptoms that are opposite of what a user would normally experience.

potency The power or strength of a drug.

prescription A message from a doctor or health care

worker that authorizes a patient to receive a certain medicine or treatment.

psychiatrist A doctor who studies, diagnoses, and treats mental illnesses, such as depression and anxiety.

psychoactive Describes a drug that affects brain function.

psychoanalysis A type of therapy during which patients talk freely about themselves.

rehab (short for rehabilitation or rehabilitate) A treatment program to help someone stop using drugs. There are many types of rehab, including inpatient programs and outpatient programs.

synthesize To make something using chemistry.

tolerance Occurs when someone needs more of a drug to achieve the same results. When someone develops a tolerance for a drug, it's easy to become addicted to it

tranquilizer A drug used to reduce anxiety, fear, tension, and similar states of mind.

trigger Something that starts something else.

withdrawal May occur if someone attempts to stop taking a drug. Symptoms of withdrawal include seizures, psychosis, severe insomnia, and severe anxiety.

Find Out More

Books

Adams, Colleen. *Rohypnol: Roofies—The Date Rape Drug*. New York: Rosen Publishing Group, 2006.

Eldridge, Alison, and Stephen Eldridge. *Investigate Club Drugs*. Berkeley Heights, NJ: 2014.

Hyde, Margaret O. *Drugs 101*. Minneapolis, MN: Twenty-First Century Books, 2003.

Kuhn, Cynthia. *Buzzed: The Straight Facts About the Most Used and Abused Drugs from Alcohol to Ecstasy*. New York: W. W. Norton & Company, 2014.

Landau, Elaine. *Date Violence*. New York: Children's Press, 2005.

Websites

Above the Influence

www.abovetheinfluence.com/drugs/rohypnol

Visit this site for facts about Rohypnol and links to information about other dangerous drugs.

Partnership for Drug-Free Kids

www.drugfree.org/drug-guide/rohypnol

Designed just for kids, this site offers information about Rohypnol as well as interesting statistics about drug use.

Substance Abuse and Mental Health Services Administration (SAMHSA) Find Help Page

www.samhsa.gov/find-help

This page offers links to local treatment centers that deal with Rohypnol abuse and addiction.

Index

Page numbers in **boldface** are illustrations. Entries in **boldface** are glossary terms.

About the Author

Kate Shoup has written more than twenty-five books and has edited hundreds more. When not working, Kate, an IndyCar fanatic, loves to ski, read, and ride her motorcycle. She lives in Indianapolis with her husband, her daughter, and their dog. To learn more about Kate and her work, visit www.kateshoup.com.